The 33 Laws of Tennis Thirty Three Concepts to Improve Your Game

By Joseph Correa

Actual professional tennis players share their trade secrets in this book

COPYRIGHT PAGE

©2013 The 33 Laws of Tennis by Joseph Correa
ISBN 978-1-941525-13-5

All rights reserved. This book or any portion thereof may not be reproduced or used in any manner without the express written permission of the publisher except for brief book quotations for reviews in the book.

Scanning, uploading, and distributing of this book via the Internet or via any other means without the express permission of the publisher and author is illegal and punishable by law.

Only purchase authorized editions of this book. Please consult with your physician before training and using this book.
You can visit the author's website at tennisvideostore.com

ABOUT THE AUTHOR

Hello, my name is Joseph Correa and I have been training and teaching tennis for over 15 years. I played professional tennis for years and am now a USPTR professional certified coach.

After years of competing and training with some of the best in the world I have learned that most people can be very successful in competition with the right mental, physical, and emotional training.

Proven scientific techniques, drills, and step by step phases must be performed to reach your peak and for that reason I have prepared the first group of training DVD's and books showing you how to reach your goals.

Through my work and teaching aids, I have helped hundreds of amateur and professional tennis player's advance with their physical, mental, and performance goals to achieve great results.

I teach you everything I know you will need to reach your goals and hope you will enjoy and share these lessons and ideas with loved ones. To learn more about the different lessons taught through my books and DVD's go to www.tennisvideostore.com. Many more books will be coming out this year with some advanced drills and techniques.

TABLE OF CONTENTS

THE 33 LAWS OF TENNIS

Law #1

"Know thy opponent"

Law #2

"The match ends, when it ends"

Law #3

"Prepare for success"

Law #4

"Keep a poker face"

Law #5

"Hide your weaknesses, exploit theirs"

Law #6

"He who gets the last ball in, wins"

Law #7

"Be true to thy self"

Law #8

"He who hits first, hits twice"

Law #9

"Be a fake to win"

Law #10

"Bring down the walls"

Law #11

"Learn from every match"

Law #12

"Acquire Knowledge"

Law #13

"Know thy rules"

Law #14

"Build your chess board"

Law #15

"Find the pattern"

Law #16

"Pawn check mates king"

Law #17

"Build a base"

Law #18

"Don't dry up the well"

Law #19

"Mind over matter"

Law #20

"Only give presents on birthdays"

Law #21

"Have the heart of a lion"

Law #22

"Choose your weapon"

Law #23

"Perfection by imitation"

Law #24

"The four leaf clover"

Law #25

"Humor for the brave"

Law #26

Go where the party is at"

Law #27

"Baby steps for giants"

Law #28

"Thy second serve: may it serve you well"

Law #29

"No jam, just bread and butter"

Law #30

"Get some wheels"

Law #31

"See the future"

Law #32

"Be the first and last"

Law #33

"See thyself"

Law #1
"Know thy opponent"

Knowing whom you are going to be up against before the match begins is extremely important. They have probably already done their homework and know more about you than you can imagine. If this is so you should go around and ask about the player you are going to be up against. You can ask friends, past opponents, team mates, anybody that can give information regarding your opponent. This information is only useful to you before the match starts, after that you will probably learn the rest on the court. Even if your opponent isn't scouting you, do your homework on him or her.

There are two main reasons why it is beneficial to scout your opponent: The first one is because you will be able to analyze his/her strengths and weaknesses. When you know this, you can decide what strategy will work best in the match. The second reason is because you will have time to rehearse the match in your mind before you even enter the tennis court. Another word also used for this kind of mental practice is "visualization". You can practice the strokes and strategies you want to use, in your mind and not get physically get tired.

High performance tennis depends greatly on this practice. Many people daydream about their match and how they are going to play and don't realize they are visualizing their game. Most of us have done it at one time or another. When you know how your opponent plays, what they like and don't like to do, their mental and physical capabilities, you can generate an accurate game plan. Mental capabilities means just how strong the mental aspect of their game is.. Physical capabilities means how well prepared they are to physically compete. Maybe your opponent is scouting you and knows how s/he will play you. He has the edge and you don't want this. The best thing you can do before a match starts is be prepared. Know your opponent.

Law #2
"The match ends, when it ends"

Matches often become contests where both players are waiting to see which one will give in first. Luckily for you a match can be won even if your one point away from losing. Many people have won after being down 6/0 6/0 0-40 deficit. This is what makes tennis so competitive. You have to be concentrated until the end of the match.

Confidence has a big role in competition, since a weak mental competitor may be ahead in a match and then lose it. Other times s/he may be down in the match and not make an effort to come back or at least give a good fight. Many players have learned not to let past circumstances affect their future matches in a negative manner. A good competitor will fight to the very end because s/he can come back and win the match despite the score. Other good competitors know how not to let an opponent back into the match and finally finish them off. Finishing a match and coming back from a deficit are some of the hardest things to accomplish in any level of play. Make sure to remind yourself that "the match ends, when it ends" so that you may become a competitor feared by others and remembered for your persistence.

APPLICATION

Practice playing from 5-0 or 4-0 up in each set and then try to finish the match. As soon as you finish your first match alternate with your practice partner as soon as you finish the first match. You should play many sets to get used to this mentality.

Law #3
"Prepare for success"

Success comes to those who are prepared for it. As in life this should be your mentality on the tennis court. Some players just put on some clothes, sun block, take some balls and a racquet, and head for the court. There they hit a couple of balls and say "serves up". Many people have only a few minutes to prepare for a practice session or match and their behavior would appear quite reasonable for the short time span available to them. Now, let's take another approach to preparation. First make a list of equipment needs and check off all the things you carry out on to the court. When you have what you physically need get mentally prepared for competition. Finally get a good warm up. This is just a general outline of a basic preparation plan. Now let's look at a specific one. These are all the basic things you will require on the court before you enter.

These are just a few. You can add more if you would like. Some of these things might seem silly but you never know how silly you will feel when you don't have them and desperately need them. Prevent from having bad moments, by having the right tools for the job. Don't be too proud to ask somebody help, even your opponent. We have all been in those painful situations and know how it feels. Most of us will gladly help each other out.

Now that you have you have your equipment ready, get your mind on the task at hand. Some people like to visualize, others get energized or pumped by talking to themselves, and many listen to music to relax. Some like to watch tennis on TV or on the court. Everybody has a different approach to get ready for a match. Sample these and other approaches to see what gets you best, mentally prepared. This is a very important part in preparation for a match. Don't take it lightly.

If you want to play tennis for many years, get a good warm up before every practice and match. You can't imagine the benefits of warming up correctly.

Start with some light stretching, this will get your muscles to become elastic. Then jog for a few minutes. You can jog in the same place or around a certain area, as long as you get your body warmed up. After this, do some mini-tennis and gradually distance yourself from the net until you get to the backcourt where you can slowly increase the speed of the ball.

Law #4
"Keep a poker face"

Most people would agree that some of the best poker players in the world are those who can keep the same face when dealt good or bad cards. This might seem strange for some to believe but it's especially true in tennis. Have you noticed how the hardest players to beat keep a straight face and show hardly and emotions or change in their gestures? This can be frustrating for people who like to see their opponents whine and throw their racquets when they perform poorly or when they lose a crucial point. Poker face players are tough competitors because they don't transmit their true feelings while on the court. Even when desperate to win, they prefer to show that necessity through concentration and calmness. Don't think they don't have emotions. They are just hidden for the moment. Try this approach to become a better competitor. Maybe you perform better when you show your emotions and that's great, but for anybody who wants to try something new, this is a good start. It can change the way you view tennis and you will start to see things you never saw before that were always present. Great things can happen when you concentrate and focus on the task at hand. When you are calm and emotionless, you greatly enhance your concentration. Keep a poker face when you play to see who is bluffing and who really has what it takes to win.

Law #5
"Hide your weaknesses, exploit theirs"

Ever notice how some players seem to be perfect on the court? Why hasn't anybody broken their game? Maybe they are very good at hiding things from others. Things they don't want you to know, like a weakness? If you don't know their weakness, where are you going to attack them? In a match, a player is at a disadvantage when s/he does not know an opponents weakness.

Before the match starts, find out what your opponent's weakness is and figure out how you can exploit it. Ask other players and friends if they know this person. You can even look on the Internet under the players name and see what helpful information is out there for you. If nobody knows this person, find out for yourself in the warm up. Hit some to their forehand, then their backhand. After that, mix up the height and spin of the ball. You will eventually find something they do poorer than the rest of their game.

For example, when you have a weak backhand, learn to run around it and hit a forehand. Another example could be if your weakness is your bad physical fitness and don't want long rallies from the baseline. In this case it is better to attack the net or keep the points short. This way your hiding your weaknesses and exploiting theirs.

APPLICATION

Have your practice partner attack your weakness with his/her weapon. At first it will feel awkward, but this will help you overcome these situations in a match. Then, have your partner hit with his/her weaker side and you with your weapon (you are simply doing the opposite). This will give a better understanding of how skillful your weapon really is and how much improvement is needed. You are learning to play defense and offense.

Law #6
"He who gets the last ball in, wins"

There are many philosophies as to how tennis should be played. The simplest possible one is "who ever gets the last ball in, wins". When the ball goes to the net or outside the singles lines, you lose the point. And when you keep the ball in, you win. This might seem very elemental, but some of the hardest things to accomplish are sometimes the elemental ones.

APPLICATION

To achieve this law, practice consistency. Get 10 balls consistently over the net and in. When you have completed 10, strive for 20. Decide what your goal will be and strive to obtain it. For example, my goal for this month is to get at least 100 balls over with my partner. When this has been achieved you can start being specific with the area, height and spin with which you hit. This will be specified in more detail in law #24.

Law #7
"Be true to thy self"

In close matches, we all get the urge to call a ball out when it is near the line. Have you heard of the saying "when in doubt, call it out"? This of course is not ethical or correct. Don't let the pressure of the moment make you be an unjust player. If it's a close call and you are not sure about it, repeat the point. It's the right thing to do. You save a lot of time and some heated arguments. Be true to yourself. Call the ball as you see it. You will feel a lot better about yourself and be respected by others.

APPLICATION

Watch a practice live match and try to call the ball in or out in your head, not out loud. This way you will practice calling close shots more often even when you are not playing. After a while you will instinctively know if a ball was good or bad.

Law #8
"He who hits first, hits twice"

Whenever you attack in a point you will be in command and will have better options to finish off the point. In other words, when you start attacking you will be able to continue to be offensive (most of the time). Don't wait for things to happen. Go out there and do your best to be the one who is in charge of the point. Learn to be proactive and not reactive. A proactive person acts in advance to deal with an expected difficulty. A reactive person responds to a stimulus. In tennis reacting to things that happen on the court is normal. When you learn to be proactive, your chances of winning increase many times over. Take control of the point. Hit first so that you may hit twice.

Law #9
"Be a fake to win"

Many people feel that they don't have the confidence or courage to win a match in pressure situations. Why not become an actor on the tennis court and play the role of the confident or courageous tennis player. Be a fake and you'll win more often than you think. Choose the way you want to be seen on and off the court. Then act like that person you want to be. You will feel a bit awkward at first, but you will get used to it with some practice. Some people don't understand the importance of the image you exert on the court.

An example of this could be if you have just played a very long first set and you are very tired. Your opponent also looks tired, but you decide to carry yourself in an energetic and positive manner. Make them think you can do this for another two sets. This can be very demoralizing for anyone. They will take one look at you and notice they have no chance (even though both of you feel just as tired inside). Your opponent decides that s/he can't handle a second set with somebody who seems not to get tired and chooses to forfeit. How about that! This does not always happen. Being a fake will surely improve your chances of winning. All actors work very hard to perfect their image. They know their success depends on it. Maybe you won't win an "Oscar" for your performance, but you'll win many more matches.

Law #10
"Bring down the walls"

Every tennis player has his/her own castle to protect. Its walls keep enemies from breaking in. But if those walls are brought down, there is very little hope for that castle. Some tennis players walls are their serve or their forehand. Others have speed or patience as their walls. When you break don a players wall you have an open gate towards attacking weaker shots. Learn to "bring down the walls" and you'll win many battles.

APPLICATION

Have your practice partner be the aggressive player and you play defensively. In other words, your practice partner will attack and try to finish the point while you just keep the ball in play waiting for him/her to miss. Once both of you get the hang of it, switch. Now you become the aggressive player and s/he becomes the defensive player. This way you will learn to bring down those walls and advance to weaker territory. Remember you are working towards disarming their weapons on way or another.

Law #11
"Learn from every match"

Mistakes are justified when you learn from them and correct them. Don't get into the habit of making unforced errors and never learning from them. This will hurt you in competitive match situations. The best way to view unforced errors is as a learning process that will take time and dedication. Keep fixing and correcting them throughout your practices and matches and watch your tennis level go up sky high. Every match tells us something. It's a waking moment. We must open our eyes and see what we need to see. So much knowledge can be accumulated through experience. Keep a log of all your experiences so that you may grow by their knowledge. Try using this sample "after match log":

After Match Log

DATE:

OPPONENT:

TOURNAMENT:

RATE YOURSELF FROM 1-10:

(10 BEING YOUR BEST PERFORMANCE)

WHAT I DID RIGHT IN THE MATCH

WHAT I DID WRONG IN THE MATCH

WHAT I LEARNED

WHAT I WILL DO TO APPLY WHAT I HAVE LEARNED

Many times we don't learn form our mistakes because we are not reminded of them. Remind yourself of all the little things you need to do to keep improving and obtaining your goals. Look through your "after match logs" at least once a weak.

Law #12
"Acquire knowledge"

Tennis Ball + Racquet + Knowledge = Success

Don't be too proud to ask for help. Many tennis instructors will be glad to help you if you ask them to. Keep in mind that some are more specialized in certain areas than others. Know what you want to improve or learn and have them help you. You'll save a lot of time learning from their errors, than by making your own errors and having to learn from them. Information on all different topics is available in tennis books, magazines, videos and on the Internet.

The more you know the more creative you can be with your tennis. You will be much better at making decisions when you have more information to decide on.

Law #13
"Know thy rules"

It's very useful to know what the rules of tennis are. Some people don't realize how many advantages can be obtained from having knowledge about:

Court dimensions

Singles rules

Doubles rules

Mixed doubles rules

Racquets

Balls

The let

Order of serve

Coaching

Wheelchair tennis rules

DID YOU KNOW?

Did you know the net is lower over the center of the court? And did you know that when you play crosscourt, you are actually hitting a high percentage shot (A shot that will have a higher percentage of going in than if you go down the line.) since the distance crosscourt is greater than the distance down the line? As you can see, the rules of tennis can be very helpful when you want to play wiser and more efficient.

APPLICATION

Obtain a copy of your tennis associations' rulebook and look over it to see how many new things you learned from it. Look at the section on the amount of time you have between points, games, sets and matches. Then take advantage of this knowledge. Practice timing yourself between points and changeovers so that you may become accustomed to the short time periods you will have in competition. Also practice playing points and then giving yourself no more then 30 seconds of rest. Work on your physical conditioning. This will help you to keep up with the rhythm you desire to maintain in a match.

Law #14
"Build your chess board"

Tennis is like a chessboard; you have to put the pieces in the all right places. When you position yourself in the right place at the right time, you find yourself hitting the ideal shot. Things don't just happen you have to make them happen. Be ready to improvise.

APPLICATION

First, work on having all the basic strokes. When you have accomplished this, mix different shots and strokes in different situations. This will help you build your game plan for each match

Practice #1
Alternate hitting topspin and backspin (slice) with your forehand. Try not to repeat the same spin twice. Only your hitting partner can hit with the same spin pattern. When you can do this well on the forehand side, do the same with the backhand. You alternate spins and your partner hits with the same spin. Then switch with your partner.

Practice #2
One player hits crosscourt while the other player hits down the line (straight). The pattern made by the strokes has the shape of an eight (8). When you are done practicing, change the patterns between you and your partner.

Law #15
"Find the pattern"

Many players are taught to play tennis in a way that can often be predictable. They learn to hit the ball to a certain place over and over. They are also taught to do certain things in specific points such as match point or set point. If you learn what their pattern is, you can predict what they will do. When you learn how to decipher a person's pattern they won't be able to surprise you. Their game will be vulnerable once you know where the ball is going and what you will do to take advantage of this situation.

You don't need to be a mathematician to learn to find patterns. Watch some tennis matches in your neighborhood or on TV. Try to find different patterns of play in each point, game, set, or even in the entire match.

Some examples of patterns are:

Crosscourt pattern   Down-the-line pattern

* Remember that every player has his or her own pattern. Some are simpler and others are more complex.

Law #16
"Pawn check mates king"

In chess, you will often find yourself in situations where you must use your weakest pieces to win. In tennis this happens often. It's very hard to wake up everyday and play your best. Once in a while, you will play a match when your tennis is not at its best and that's when it counts the most to bring out the champion in you. Winning when your are performing at lower level of tennis than your used to is quite a challenge, but this is where you separate yourself from the rest. Be victorious in the best and worst of times.

APPLICATION

Play a match where your practice partner attacks your weakness with his/her weapon. Do this for no more than forty-five minutes and then switch. After both of you have completed at least two sets, play some practice points in which you can hit anywhere you like and see how comfortable you now feel when you have to come up with big shots with your weaker side.

Play a competitive match with someone other than your practice partner. Compare your performance to that of past matches where your weakness was the cause of your loss. You will notice that you have a lot more confidence in your weaker side then before. This will help you win tough matches even when you are not playing your best. There are other techniques that can be used for different circumstances, but this is a good start.

Law #17
"Build a base"

In life, we usually have different plans for the same objectives. We have plan A and if plan A doesn't get the job done, we use plan B. When plan B can't get the job done, we use plan C. This is called building a strategic base. In tennis you might have to change your game plans many times in a single match. It is wise to have a base strategy or a strategy, which we think is best, suited for the opponent you are up against. Build a base and when you have done this, think of alternative strategies that can be used if anything goes wrong.

Obviously, you will have plan A that is your best game strategy or the game your most comfortable with. Now you need to decide what is going to be your plan B. If your plan A is based on pounding winners from the baseline, your plan B could be attacking the net. That way you speed up the rhythm of play. Finally, plan C might just be keeping the ball in play and waiting for your opponent to make the errors. This will slow down your rhythm of play.

If something doesn't work for you, try going from your plan A to plan B. If plan B is not the solution, try plan C. Always have at least three alternative strategies you can fall back on, but first build a base. Your base is the plan with which you start every match. It is usually the one that has given you the best results in the past and which you feel most comfortable with.

Law #18
"Don't dry up the well"

The most logical way to win is through the use of your weapon/s. But when you use a weapon much too often your opponent becomes accustomed to it. This becomes dangerous for you. It's good to keep opponents guessing. Use your weapon as much as possible but mix up some other shots to keep them off balance. Don't let them get used to seeing the same pattern or the same stroke much too often. Don't dry up the well. Become unpredictable.

APPLICATION

A good way to learn or improve the way you mix up your shots is by being specific in your practice. Play some points with your practice partner where neither of you are not allowed to hit the same shot twice. At first, do this without serving. Just start the point with an underhand toss. An example of this drill could be:

Hit a forehand:

With topspin

With slice

Flat

Deep into the court with topspin

Short into the court with topspin

Deep into the court with slice

Short into the court with slice

Hit a backhand:

With topspin

With slice

Flat

Deep into the court with topspin

Short into the court with topspin

Deep into the court with slice

Short into the court with slice

NOTE: Shots can be repeated as long as they are alternated with another stroke. You can make it as simple as you want. When you become skillful you can add as many different shots as you want. It is best to start mixing two or three different shots and gradually add more with time.

Law #19
"Mind over matter"

Tennis starts as a physical game but then transcends into a more mental game. Things that our physical body can't do, our mind can do many times over. The power of the mind is unimaginable. Emotions and thoughts become extremely important when we get nervous or uncomfortable in competition. Our body will do things we sometimes wonder. "Why didn't I just lift my arm a little higher and get the ball over the net?" What we have to remember is that our mind controls our body and it is just doing what our mind has told it to do. Work on controlling your emotions. They can become great allies in times of need. Concentration is basic in competition. It is a great skill that can be learned with some practice. It is one of the hardest things to master, but very valuable indeed.

Law #20
"Only give presents on birthdays"

Most of us know how important it is not to give up any points in a match and especially when it is a close one. We often give away some presents that eventually hurt us in the long run. Minimize those presents or unforced errors when competing. Only give presents on birthdays.

APPLICATION

An excellent way to minimize presents is by improving your consistency. The next time you step on the tennis court after you've warmed up, take just one ball out and keep that ball in play with your practice partner for as long as possible. You want to accustom yourself to keep the ball in play right from the first point. When you practice this, count how many times you get the ball in without missing. When you have missed that first ball after maintaining it in play for a while, choose a specific side, stroke and spin with which you want to hit and do the same consistency exercise. For example: Hit crosscourt forehands with topspin. Try to keep the ball in play for as long as possible without missing and then write down the amount of times the ball went in. Do this for each side you practice (forehand and backhand) and compare it with your next days practice. You should at least do this with these exercises: crosscourt forehands, crosscourt backhands, forehand backhand down the line and backhand forehand down the line.

Law #21
"Have the heart of a lion"

Tennis matches and tournaments are won in many ways. Some are won, by having an extraordinary skill. Others are won, by being in better physical condition than the rest. The way specified in this law is probably the most important and least paid attention to HEART. It has the power to bring our level of tennis to a perfect ten. It can make you become feared amongst competitors. Most important of all, it will make you victorious.

Law #22
"Choose your weapon"

When you start to improve your level of tennis, you will feel more in control. This control is the beginning of your specialization. Everybody has something they do better than the rest. This is what allows you to control the point through one or all of these: power, placement, spin, and consistency. This is called your "weapon". The more you improve your weapon, the more dangerous you'll become. Some players have unpredictable serves. Others have powerful forehands or backhands. Many win with their speed and athleticism. Find your weapon and when you do, enhance it's potential by creating another weapon. That way you'll have two weapons and become a double threat for others.

Law #23
"Perfection by imitation"

Some of the greatest artists of all time began by imitating their favorite painters and then went on to create their own style and form of art. Creating your own style of play is also a wonderful thing to do but this might take some time. Tennis can also be imitated and then perfected. Look for a specific professional tennis player who has the style of play you desire. Then read about him/her. Watch their matches on TV. Try to mimic their every detail, until you master their style of play. When you do, make it your own by adjusting it until you feel comfortable. Remember, don't become a copy of another tennis player, just take what they do best and make it better.

Law #24
"The four leaf clover"

Four-leaf clovers, a lucky rabbits foot, horseshoes are all forms of good luck charms and they all bring you good luck. Is luck important in tennis? Yes. Why? Well, because there are just things that we cannot control no matter what we do. Can we let luck be the deciding factor in the result of our match? No. We must improve our chances by doing the right things like: prepare correctly for a match, analyze opponents, use adequate strategies, be positive and stay focused. These are just a few, but it's a beginning. Luck comes to those who look for it. Don't wait for the right moment or the right match to play your true potential. Do it right now. Start with the very first point and continue until the end of the match. You will know which matches or points are the result of luck. Those points didn't come without a little hard work.

APPLICATION:

Make your own luck and see the results. The best way to make your own luck is through goal setting. Choose goals that can be measured. That way you can see your improvement and decide if changes need to be made to your goals. Once you know what these goals are decide how you are going to achieve them and write it down. Then, make daily goals that will help you achieve your main goals.

Write down your daily goals on an index card and carry

it everywhere you go. Every time your about to do something ask yourself: "Is this getting me closer to my goal?" If it isn't, then stop doing it. If it is, then your on your way to success.

This is a simple example:

Your goal may be: "improve my first serve percentage by 20%."

Now decide what you need to do to make this reality:

Have an expert take a look at my serve.

Practice "X" amount of serves per week.

Put more spin on the ball.

Improve my acceleration.

Increase leg strength.

Use targets in my practice (cones, balls, etc)

Now turn these ideas into daily goals and write them down on an index card so that you can check them many times a day.

Law #25
"Humor for the brave"

When you are in tight matches and things aren't going the way you would like them to, you tend to get cranky, negative and careless. How do some players use these moments to make themselves stronger? Most of the careless mistakes you make in important points occur because of the pressure that you feel. A great way to get rid of that pressure is through humor. Whenever you make a silly mistake laugh at it. You can't imagine how relaxed you'll feel and how this can positively affect your game. When you are in a good mood, most things tend to go the way you want them to. Yes, you still want to win and still feel the pressure, but smiling or laughing at these mistakes can keep you competitive. When you are competitive you fight till the end and everyone can feel it. Don't take the easy way out yelling and throwing your racket. You'll enjoy tennis more if you laugh at the bad moments and continue to the good ones.

Law #26
"Go where the party is at"

When you feel that practicing with your tennis buddies or at a certain training facility is just not good enough any more. If you are not improving your level of play the way you'd like to or simply want to start competing on a regular basis, go where the party is. In other words, go where you can train the way you would like to or go where you may compete with whom you want. If you keep doing the same things, you'll keep getting the same results. It's up to you. What do you want to do with your tennis? Go where you need to be.

Law #27
"Baby steps for giants"

True champions know that it takes time to become great. It all starts with those few steps and continues with more small steps, not leaps. Everything you do will seem effortless when you take your time. First you learn how to drive at 10mph. Then you learn to go a bit faster say 25mph. Later you go to 50mph. Finally after successive baby steps, you get to 100mph. The same thing applies in tennis. Don't get frustrated with slow improvements as long as they are gradual. These small improvements are the seed for future growth. Want to become a tennis giant? Then take baby steps to success.

Law #28
"Thy second serve: may it serve you well"

The second serve can make you or break you as a tennis player. A good second serve will get you some easy points or at least put you in a good position to start the point. A bad second serve will make you double fault often and will permit your opponent to control the point right from the start. Practice these useful drills to increase your second serve percentage.

Law #29
"No jam, just bread and butter"

Learn to have keystrokes and key shots that you will use in critical situations. Under pressure situations our mind and body try to get the job done together, but sometimes they over do it. When our mind has to make critical decisions in short amounts of time it might not always make the right decisions. It is crucial in tennis to make pinpoint accurate decisions even if we have short amounts of times. A wonderful way to help our mind make decisions in short time spans is by predetermining what we will do when we are in a pressure situation.

An example of a predetermined shot would be if you decided that when you needed a specific point, you would hit an approach shot and rush to the net. Since this is where you feel most comfortable and might exert the most amount of pressure.

Another example of a predetermined shot would be if you opened up the court with a wide shot and then finished the point by hitting to the open court. There are many straegies available. The most important thing to do is know beforehand what we will do when we need to perform, or what shot we will hit in a specific situation. This way our mind can freely do its job and won't have to overanalyze anything.

Law #30
"Get some wheels"

Fast, flexible and powerful legs are crucial in tennis. They get you there and help you to prepare for the shot. Pay attention to them. Have you ever noticed that tennis is a sport that requires a lot of running? What would happen if you were twice as fast? Could you get to the ball twice as fast? The power of your strokes comes from your legs. This is your base, where your stroke begins and ends.

Law #31
"See the future"

Learn to anticipate your opponents' game, pattern and tempo. Try moving before things happen. Look for signs. Some people think that you need to be lighting-fast on the court, but they don't understand that speed can be improved by enhancing their ability to anticipate.

Law #32
"Be the first and last"

Be the first to come on the court and the last to leave. If you want to be better than the rest, train a little more than the average players. In match situations, come early and prepare before you perform and after the match is over, spend that extra time on the court reflecting on how the match or practice went.

Law #33
"See thyself"

Most of you will never know how you actually play. You hear all kinds of comments on how you play and probably have a vague perception of what you must look like on the court, but don't really see yourself. The only way to know how you play is by seeing yourself. This can be done by having someone film you when you are playing and then play it back to see the "real you". A cell phone or video camcorder will do the job. If you don't have one, borrow one. Many truths become apparent when this is done. You can't imagine what an impact it can have on your tennis life. It will change the way you see yourself forever. Have someone tape you from different angles and distances, so that you may have a better perspective. See thyself!

@ The 33 Laws of Tennis By Joseph Correa

Good luck in your matches. This book will help you win more matches.

For more great tennis videos and books, check out www.tennisvideostore.com

There you will find titles such as:

Tennis Footwork Training by Joseph Correa

Yoga Tennis by Joseph Correa

The 33 Laws of Tennis by Joseph Correa

Tennis Abs by Joseph Correa

32 Tennis Strategies for Today's Game by Joseph Correa

WOULD YOU DO ME A FAVOR?

Thank you for downloading and reading this book. I hope it was helpful and at least one thing makes you win an extra match or two.

I have a small favor to ask. Would you mind writing a short comment and rate this book.

I like to read all the reviews on my books and enjoy knowing what others think of this book. I feel the best pay comes from good positive reviews from tennis enthusiasts that enjoyed reading it.

If you know of a family member or friend, that you think would benefit from reading this book, please take a minute to share it with them so that they may improve their game as well. I enjoy helping others and would like to answer questions free of charge. You can Tweet me on www.twitter.com at @mybetterswing.com
Check out some of my other books on the next page.

OTHER TITLES BY JOSEPH CORREA

Tennis Serve Harder Training Program
This DVD will teach you how to serve 10-20 mph faster in a 3 month day by day program. The best serve training program in the market. Video includes a 3 month chart training program and a step by step manual. The DVD shows you how to do the exercises properly and the process you should follow in order to be successful with the program.

Joseph Correa is a professional tennis player and coach that has competed and taught all over the world in ITF and ATP tournaments for many years. Besides being a professional tennis player he has a USPTR professional coaching certification and ITF kids coaching certification.

The 33 Laws of Tennis
The 33 Laws of Tennis is book full of valuable tennis concepts to help you become a better and more prepared tennis player. Written by a professional tennis player and coach in the USA. It's a very useful book that will come in handy when you least expect it and will remind you of many little but important things before competing.

Tennis Footwork and Cardio by Joseph Correa
Joseph Correa is a professional tennis player and coach that has competed and taught all over the world in ITF and ATP tournaments for many years. Besides being a professional tennis player he has a USPTR professional coaching certification and ITF kids coaching certification.

Get in better shape and improve your mobility on and off the tennis court. Your foot work will improve drastically as well as strengthen your core and upper body. This is definitely worthwhile for a serious tennis player no matter what your level. You become faster, stronger, and more agile and on the court as well as seeing an increase in acceleration in your groundstrokes and serve. Created by a professional tennis player for others to advance in their game and win more matches.

Yoga Tennis by Joseph Correa
Yoga Tennis by Joseph Correa is a great way to improve your flexibility and agility on the court. Reach more balls and have fewer injuries. It's a great way to win more by working on a different part of your game. The DVD lasts about 30 minutes. Used by amateur and professional tennis players to improve their game and last longer in matches. This is the best way for a tennis player to become more flexible and get rid of common back, knee, shoulder, hamstring, calf, and quadriceps injuries. You´ll be glad to get started! This is an improved version of our MBS Yoga Tennis 2012.

The Vilcabamba Diet
The best diet and exercise book you will find if you want to get in shape and live longer. It's based on a village in Ecuador called "Vilcabamba" where most of its inhabitants live longer than the average person and in great condition. Great for athletes!

Tennis Abs by Joseph Correa
Tennis Abs is a great way to strengthen your core for more powerful serves, forehands and backhands as well as stronger volleys. Abdominals are fundamental

for a better game. This DVD works on many types of crunches, sit-ups, and lateral abs and back exercises that you won´t find in other abdominal videos. Feel confident when changing your shirt during your match and hit the ball harder!

12 Tennis Secrets to Win More

By Joseph Correa

What you should be doing and working on to win all the time

32 Tennis Strategies For Today's Game

By Joseph Correa

Win more matches and tournaments with these valuable strategies for all levels!

54 TENNIS DRILLS FOR TODAY'S GAME:
IMPROVE CONSISTENCY AND POWER

"This book will teach you how to become more consistent by adding spin to your shots which will give you the confidence to hit with more power."

By Joseph Correa

60 Tennis Strategies and Mental Tactics:

Mental Toughness Training

By Joseph Correa

114 Tennis Strategies, Mental Tactics, and Drills

Improve Your Game In 10 Days

By Joseph Correa

AB TRAINING
By Joseph Correa©

Ab training for athletes of all levels!

1 DVD

MBS
YOGA TENNIS 2012©

By
Joseph Correa

This video will improve your flexibility, agility and balance on and off the court with some awsome results. Used by professional tennis players and amateurs.

1 DVD

THE VILCABAMBA DIET

Learn how to live longer and healthier like the people of Vilcabamba!

This book includes:
101 Exercises You Can Do Any Time & Any Place plus BONUS ABS

By
Joseph G. Correa

In Collaboration With
Dr. Juan Carlos Correa

CARDIO TENNIS AND ABS

By Joseph Correa©

This video will improve your flexibility, agility and balance on and off the court with some awsome results. Used by professional tennis players and amateurs.

1 DVD

Complete Tennis and Serve Conditioning by Joseph Correa

Improve your serve, foot speed, and agility with these videos that will get you winning more matches than ever before.

1 DVD

Tennis Fitness:

Tennis Abs, Yoga Tennis, and Serve Training

By Joseph Correa

Improve your serve, speed, and flexibility with this combination of footwork and stretches that will get you winning more matches than ever before.

1 DVD

Fit For Tennis:
Tennis Abs and Yoga Tennis

By Joseph Correa

Improve your serve, speed, and flexibility with this combination of footwork and stretches that will get you winning more matches than ever before.

1 DVD

Fit For Tennis:
Yoga Tennis, Serve Dynamics, and Serve Training
By Joseph Correa

Improve your serve, speed, and flexibility with this combination of footwork and stretches that will get you winning more matches than ever before.

1 DVD

Fit For Tennis:

Yoga Tennis and Serve Training

By Joseph Correa

Improve your serve, speed, and flexibility with this combination of footwork and stretches that will get you winning more matches than ever before.

1 DVD

Les 33 Lois Du Tennis

Par Joseph Correa

Comment améliorer votre jeu en trente trois concepts

Serve Harder Training Program
Pocket Manual
By Joseph Correa

**Serve 10 to 20 mph faster in 90 days!
Includes 3 training charts
and the training Manual.**

SERVE HARDER TRAINING PROGRAM BY JOSEPH CORREA©

**Serve 10 to 20 mph faster in 90 days!
Includes 3 training charts
and the training Manual.**

1 DVD

Singles and Doubles Tennis Strategies:

Winning Tactics and Mental Strategies to Beat Anyone

By Joseph Correa

Superman Tennis Serve

Learn how to serve your fastest serve ever through scientifically proven techniques!

By Joseph Correa

Tennis Abs
By Joseph Correa©

Tennis Abs are a series of abdominal exercises that will help you improve your core strength and overall performance on and off the court.

1 DVD

Tennis Conditioning:
Cardio Tennis, Serve Dynamics, and Serve Training

By Joseph Correa

Improve your serve, speed, and flexibility with this combination of footwork and stretches that will get you winning more matches than ever before.

1 DVD

Tennis Conditioning:
Cardio Tennis and Serve Dynamics

By Joseph Correa

Improve your serve, speed, and flexibility with this combination of footwork and stretches that will get you winning more matches than ever before.

1 DVD

Tennis Conditioning:
Cardio Tennis and Serve Training

By Joseph Correa

Improve your serve, speed, and flexibility with this combination of footwork and stretches that will get you winning more matches than ever before.

DVD

Tennis Conditioning:
Cardio Tennis, Yoga Tennis, Serve Dynamics, and Serve Training
By Joseph Correa

Improve your serve, speed, and flexibility with this combination of footwork and stretches that will get you winning more matches than ever before.

DVD

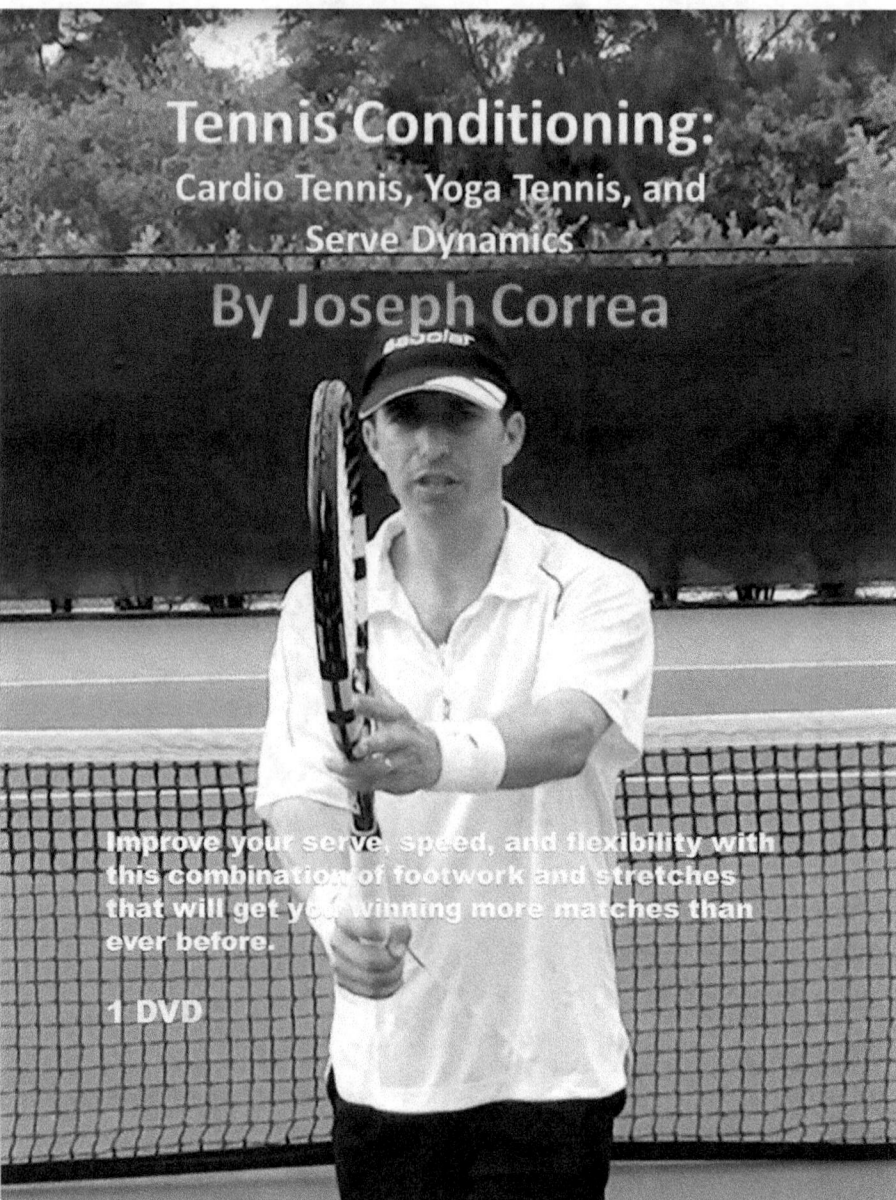

Tennis Conditioning:
Cardio Tennis, Yoga Tennis, and Serve Training

By Joseph Correa

Improve your serve, speed, and flexibility with this combination of footwork and stretches that will get you winning more matches than ever before.

1 DVD

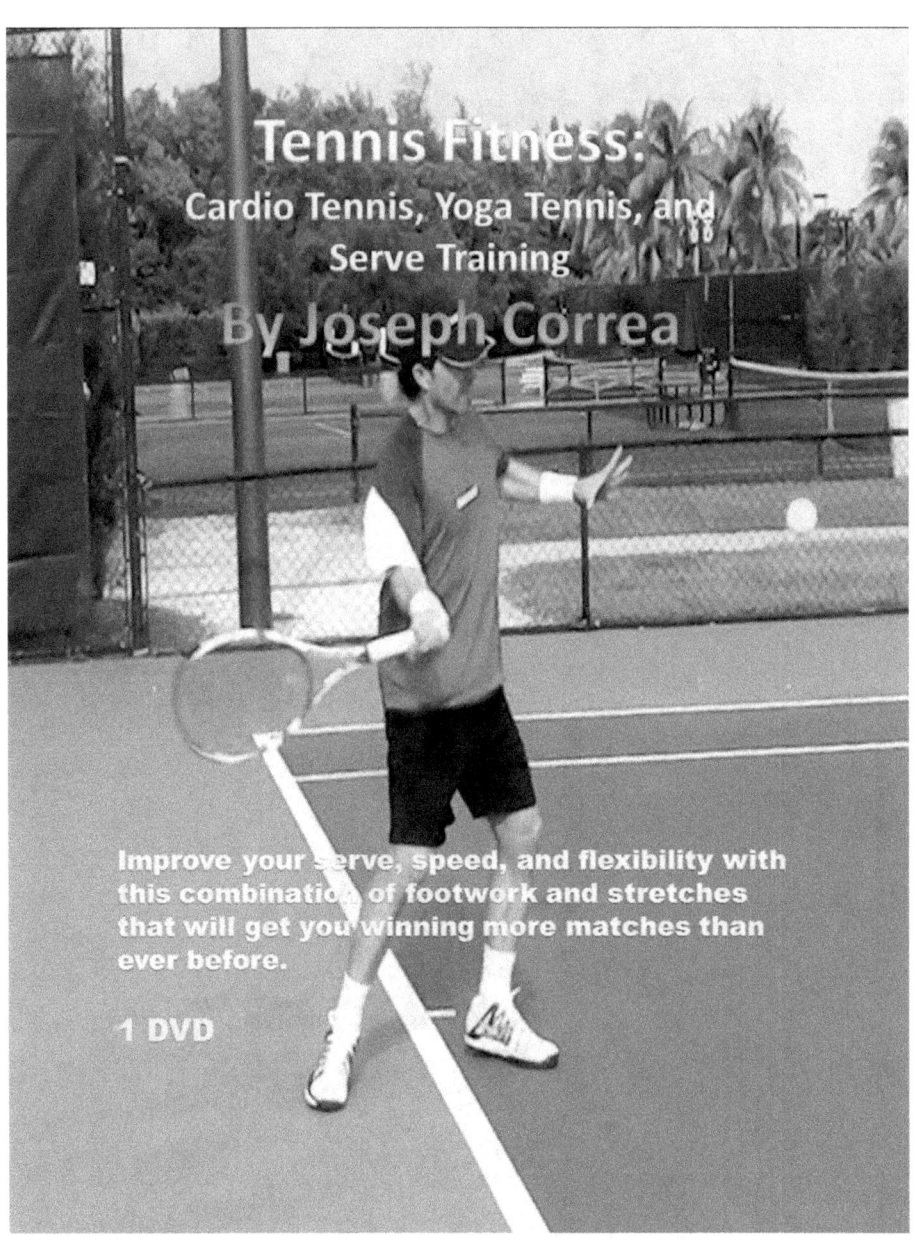

Tennis Training:
Tennis Abs, Yoga Tennis, and Serve Training

Improve your serve, speed, and flexibility with this combination of footwork and stretches that will get you winning more matches than ever before.

1 DVD

By Joseph Correa

TENNIS FOOTWORK AND CARDIO

BY JOSEPH CORREA©

This video will improve your flexibility, agility and balance on and off the court with some awsome results. Used by professional tennis players and amateurs.

1 DVD

SERVE HARDER TRAINING PROGRAM

TENNIS

MANUAL

Coach Joseph Correa

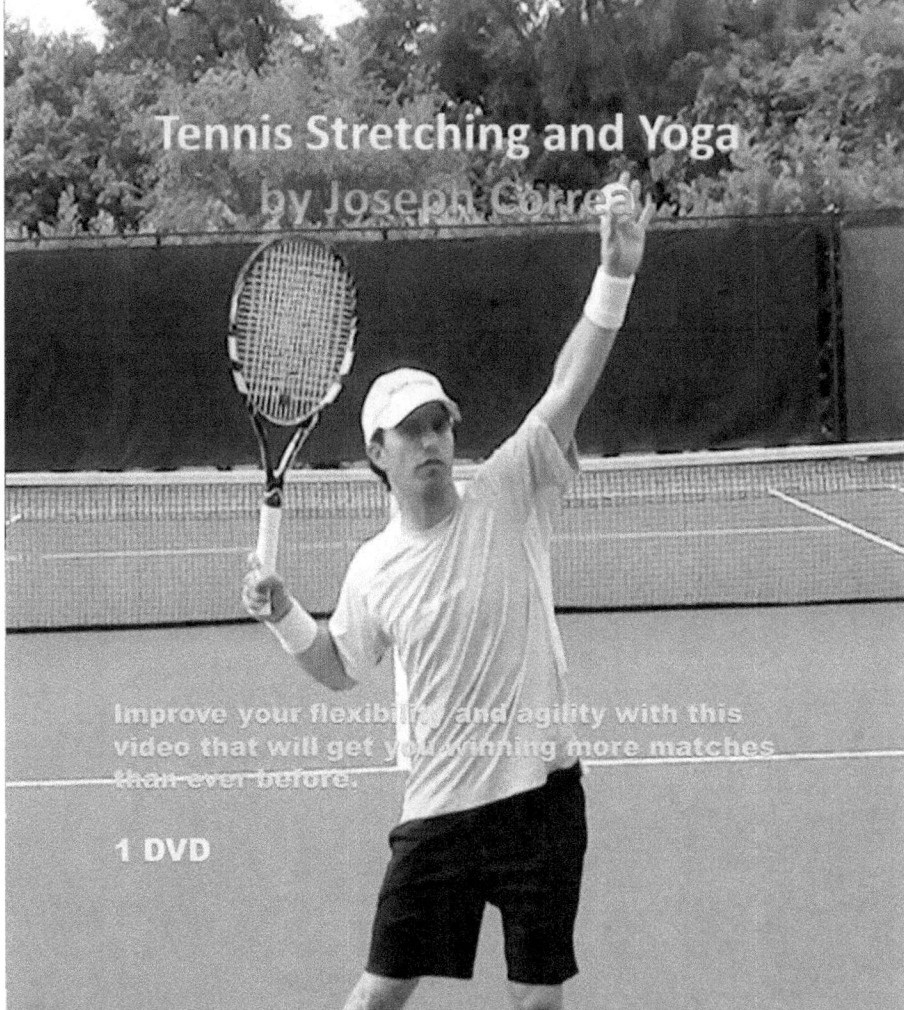

Tennis Training:
Tennis Abs, Cardio Tennis, and Serve Dynamics

Improve your serve, speed, and flexibility with this combination of footwork and stretches that will get you winning more matches than ever before.

1 DVD

By Joseph Correa

Tennis Training:
Tennis Abs and Serve Dynamics

Improve your serve, speed, and flexibility with this combination of footwork and stretches that will get you winning more matches than ever before.

1 DVD

By Joseph Correa

Tennis Training:
Tennis Abs and Serve Training

Improve your serve, speed, and flexibility with this combination of footwork and stretches that will get you winning more matches than ever before.

1 DVD

By Joseph Correa

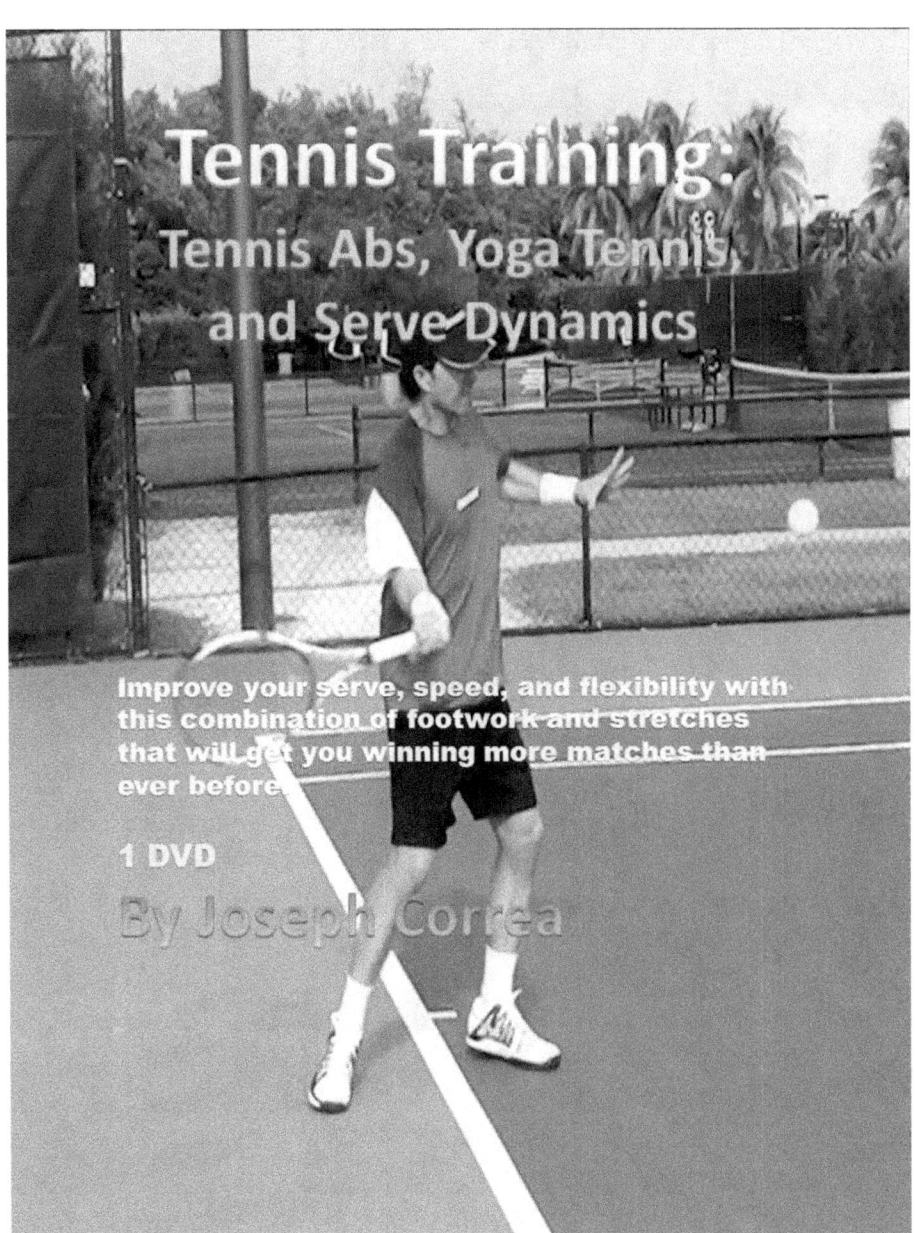

Tennis Training:

Yoga Tennis and Serve Dynamics

Improve your serve, speed, and flexibility with this combination of footwork and stretches that will get you winning more matches than ever before.

1 DVD

By Joseph Correa

DR. JUAN CARLOS CORREA and JOSEPH CORREA

The Vilcabamba Diet :

Lose 10 pounds or more!

Lose Weight, Live Longer, and Eat Healthier with the Magic Formula of our Ancestors

Women's Tennis Strategies:

Win More Matches by Playing Smarter

by Joseph Correa

The Best Tennis Strategies to Win More!